DOGS SET III

Siberian Huskies

Bob Temple

ABDO Publishing Company

visit us at
www.abdopub.com

Published by ABDO Publishing Company, 4940 Viking Drive, Suite 622, Edina, Minnesota 55435.

Printed in the United States

Edited by: Paul Joseph

Photo credits: Peter Arnold, Inc.; Ron Kimball Photography

Library of Congress Cataloging-in-Publication Data

Temple, Bob.
        Siberian huskies / Bob Temple
                p. cm. — (Dogs. Set III)
        ISBN 1-57765-420-X
        1. Siberian husky—Juvenile literature. [1. Siberian husky. 2. Dogs. 3. Pets] I. Title.

SF429.S65 T36 2000
636.73—dc21
                              00-036188

Contents

Where Dogs Come From

Dogs and humans have lived together for many years. Today, millions of dogs serve as family pets. Some of these dogs have jobs to do, too. They might help with hunting or live on a farm and help herding the other animals.

Dogs work in other ways, too. In colder climates, some dogs help people by pulling sleds, even today. The Siberian Husky is one such dog.

You may have heard of dogs being called "canines." This is because they are from a species of animal called Canidae, from the Latin word canis, which means "dog." Some wild animals, like wolves and foxes, are members of this family.

Opposite page: The Siberian Husky is related to the wolf.

Siberian Husky

Siberian Huskies are from the Working group of dogs. This means that they serve a purpose for humans. Many Siberian Huskies are nothing more than **companion** dogs for their owners. But some Siberian Huskies also work on sled teams and compete in races. They even go on long sledding treks in very cold weather, helping explorers get to places like the North Pole!

Siberian Huskies started in Siberia, one of the coldest places in the world. They were brought to Alaska in 1909 by fur traders and were often used in sled-dog races. They became famous in 1925, when there was an outbreak of the disease called diphtheria in Nome, Alaska. Teams of Siberian Huskies helped save the lives of many people by delivering medicine from other cities.

Siberian Huskies are very active dogs. They work on sled teams and even compete in races.

What They're Like

Siberian Huskies make great family pets, especially in colder weather. They are gentle and playful. They are very good with children and friendly with strangers. In fact, they are so friendly that they don't make very good watchdogs.

Because this breed is used to pulling sleds, Siberian Huskies need a lot of exercise. They are best off in a place where they have lots of room to run. However, they should not be outside in very hot weather for long periods of time.

Most of all, Siberian Huskies love to pull things. In areas where there is no snow, many people will harness their Siberian Husky to a wagon or cart and have them pull that. Nothing makes the Siberian Husky happier.

Opposite page: Siberian Huskies love to be outside.

Coat and Color

Siberian Huskies have two different **coats**. The outer coat is straight, silky, and smooth. Under that is a very soft, thick undercoat. Because of this, it is able to work in temperatures as low as –60 degrees F (-51 C).

The color can be anything from very white to mostly black. They often have special markings on their faces, especially between their eyes. Their eyes can be either brown or blue. In fact, some Siberian Huskies have one of each.

Opposite page: Most Siberian Huskies have special markings on their face.

Size

The Siberian Husky grows to be between 20 and 23 inches (51 to 58 cm) tall at the shoulders. They usually weigh between 35 and 60 pounds (16 to 27 kg). The males are usually bigger than the females.

Their bodies are very strong and muscular. Their heads are round and their **muzzle** is thin. Their ears point up. They have a bushy tail that looks very much like a wolf's.

Opposite page: The Siberian Husky is very strong and muscular.

Care

Siberian Huskies shed regularly and need to be brushed at least once a day. A wire brush or a metal comb are the best tools for taking care of the fur. Your dog's ears, teeth, and nails should be checked at least once a month.

Siberian Huskies can live inside or outside. They are too big to be kept in an apartment. If they are left outside, they should have a doghouse with a warm bed for them to sleep in. If they are kept in a fenced yard or kennel, you should make sure the fence is secure. Some Siberian Huskies will dig out under a fence and crawl out.

If the weather gets very warm, your Siberian Husky will be happier in an air-conditioned house. If you decide to keep your Siberian Husky outside, you should make sure he still gets plenty of attention from your family. All dogs need lots of love to be happy and healthy.

You should make sure to take your dog to the **veterinarian** at least once a year to get the shots he needs. These shots keep him from getting diseases that are dangerous to dogs, like **distemper** and **rabies**.

Siberian Huskies can live either inside or outside.

Feeding

Good **nutrition** is important for all dogs. Even though they are hard-working dogs, Siberian Huskies don't eat as much as many other big dogs. As puppies, they usually get fed twice a day.

Once they become adult dogs, they usually only need to eat once per day. Because Siberian Huskies don't usually overeat, many people just leave food out for them all day long. Of course, your dog needs plenty of clean, fresh water, too.

When you first get your puppy, it's a good idea to keep feeding it the same food the breeder used. This will help keep your puppy's stomach from getting upset. Your **veterinarian** can give you advice on what kind of food to use.

Opposite page: Siberian Huskies need a proper diet to stay healthy and happy.

Things They Need

Siberian Huskies love to run and to pull things. They need plenty of exercise, but you have to be careful in hot weather. Because of their thick fur, they can get overheated. They also love to play fetch or to go jogging with you. If you live in a snowy climate, you should get a harness for your Siberian Husky. You can hook it up to a sled and take a ride.

Because they love to run so much, it's important for your Siberian Husky to get obedience training. That will keep him from running away.

Your dog should always wear a collar with an identification tag that includes your name, address, and telephone number. This way, you can be called if your dog runs off. Some cities require dogs to have a **license**, too.

Opposite page: The Siberian Husky needs a lot of exercise.

Puppies

Siberian Huskies have **litters** of six to eight puppies. When they are first born, the puppies look like cuddly little bears. Like all dogs, Siberian Huskies are **mammals**. This means they will drink milk from their mother's body for the first few weeks of their lives. After about four weeks, you can begin **weaning**. At this time, you give them soft puppy food to eat.

They should get a lot of attention from humans early in their lives to help them get used to it. Puppies need a series of shots early in their lives. You should make sure you get your puppy to the **veterinarian** soon after you get him. If he stays healthy, your Siberian Husky can live 12 to 15 years.

Opposite page: Siberian Husky puppies need a lot of attention from humans.

Glossary

coat: the hair that covers a dog's body.

companion: one that keeps company with another; a friend.

distemper: a contagious disease that dogs sometimes get. It is caused by a virus.

license (LIE-sense): a tag worn by a dog indicating it has been registered with a city.

litter: the group of puppies a dog has in one pregnancy.

mammal: warm-blooded animals that feed their babies milk from the mother's body.

muzzle: the jaws and nose of a dog; snout.

nutrition (new-TRISH-un): food; nourishment.

rabies: a serious virus that is very dangerous to dogs.

veterinarian (VET-er-in-AIR-ian): your dog's doctor; also called a vet.

weaning: learning to eat food that is not from the mother.

Internet Sites

Everything Husky
http://www.yukonalaska.com/husky/index.html
Information on all types of outdoor activities you can participate in with your Siberian Husky. Learn about mushing, skijoring, and more. This includes information on other, similar breeds. It includes links to Husky organizations, nutritional information, and other resources.

The Siberian Husky Club of America, Inc.
http://www.shca.org
Information on sled-dog racing, and links to events around the country are available here. There are also guidelines for buying and selling Siberian Husky puppies and adult dogs. Health information and a history of the breed are also available.

Index